WELCOME TO THE U.S.A.
HAWAI`I

Written by Ann Heinrichs   Illustrated by Matt Kania
Content Adviser: Nanette Napoleon,
Cultural Consultant, Kailua, Hawai`i

The Child's World

J 919.69
Heinrichs

Published in the United States of America by The Child's World®
PO Box 326 • Chanhassen, MN 55317-0326
800-599-READ • www.childsworld.com

Photo Credits

Cover: Photodisc; frontispiece: Brand X Pictures.

Interior: Aloha Festivals: 10; Corbis: 6 (Roger Ressmeyer), 13 (Douglas Peebles), 14 (Lucy Pemoni/Reuters), 15 (Richard Cummins), 17 (Phil Shermeister), 29 (James L. Amos), 33 (David Pu'u), 34 (Dave G. Houser), 35; Dole Plantation: 25; Gay & Robinson Tour: 18; Getty Images: 19 (Hulton|Archive), 22 (Taxi/Lisa Romerein), 26 (Ronen Zilberman); Photodisc: 30; Polynesian Cultural Center: 21; Brenda Zaun/US Fish & Wildlife Service: 9.

Acknowledgments

The Child's World®: Mary Berendes, Publishing Director

Editorial Directions, Inc.: E. Russell Primm, Editorial Director; Katie Marsico, Associate Editor; Judith Shiffer, Assistant Editor; Matt Messbarger, Editorial Assistant; Susan Hindman, Copy Editor; Melissa McDaniel, Proofreader; Peter Garnham, Matt Messbarger, Olivia Nellums, Chris Simms, Molly Symmonds, Katherine Trickle, Carl Stephen Wender, Fact Checkers; Tim Griffin/IndexServ, Indexer; Cian Loughlin O'Day, Photo Researcher and Editor

The Design Lab: Kathleen Petelinsek, Design and art production

Library of Congress Cataloging-in-Publication Data
Heinrichs, Ann.
  Hawai'i / by Ann Heinrichs.
    p. cm. — (Welcome to the U.S.A.)
  Includes index.
  ISBN 1-59296-374-9 (library bound : alk. paper) 1. Hawaii—Juvenile literature.
2. Hawaii—Geography—Juvenile literature. I. Title. II. Series.
  DU623.25.H453 2006
  996.9—dc22   2004026164

Ann Heinrichs is the author of more than 100 books for children and young adults. She has also enjoyed successful careers as a children's book editor and an advertising copywriter. Ann grew up in Fort Smith, Arkansas, and lives in Chicago, Illinois.

About the Author
Ann Heinrichs

Matt Kania loves maps and, as a kid, dreamed of making them. In school he studied geography and cartography, and today he makes maps for a living. Matt's favorite thing about drawing maps is learning about the places they represent. Many of the maps he has created can be found in books, magazines, videos, Web sites, and public places.

About the
Map Illustrator
Matt Kania

On the cover: Breathtaking cliffs are part of Maui's coastline.
On page one: There are 9 telescopes at the Mauna Kea observatories.

OUR HAWAI`I TRIP

Are you ready to explore the Aloha State? Then hop aboard. We're heading out to Hawai'i!

You'll surf ocean waves. You'll learn a new way to crack nuts. You'll even climb a **volcano** and eat roasted pig.

Does that sound like fun? Then buckle up and hang on tight. We're off!

WELCOME TO HAWAI'I

Many Hawaiian words have diacritics, or special marks. One is the 'okina ('). It tells you to stop the breath quickly in your throat. The kahakō, or macron (¯), means you should make a vowel sound longer.

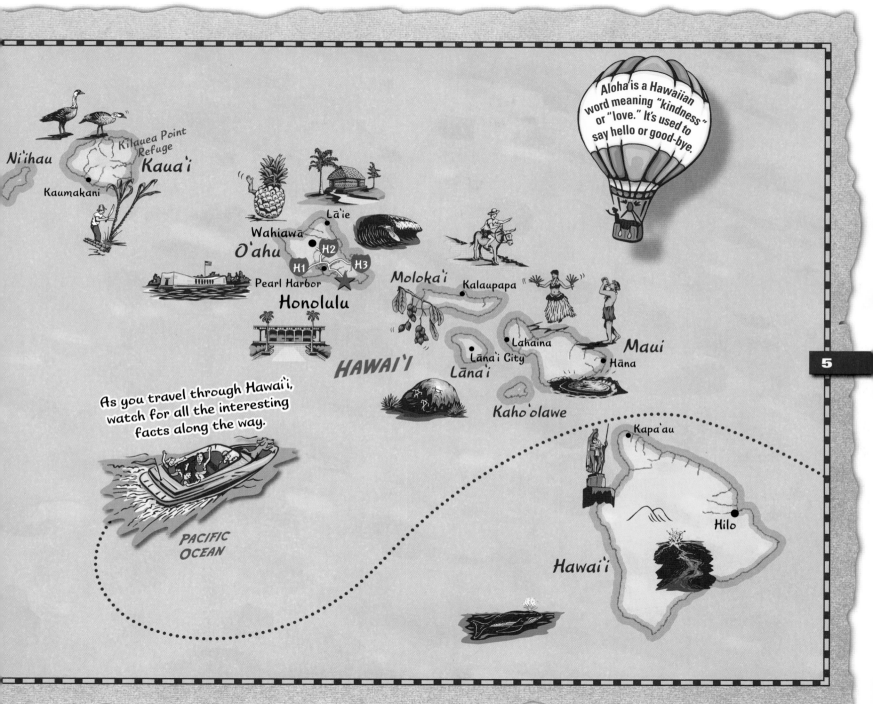

Ni'ihau

Kaumakani

Kilauea Point Refuge

Kaua'i

Wahiawa

La'ie

O'ahu

H1 H2 H3

Pearl Harbor

Honolulu

HAWAI'I

Moloka'i

Kalaupapa

Lahaina

Lāna'i City

Lāna'i

Kaho'olawe

Maui

Hāna

Aloha is a Hawaiian word meaning "kindness" or "love." It's used to say hello or good-bye.

As you travel through Hawai'i, watch for all the interesting facts along the way.

PACIFIC OCEAN

Kapa'au

Hilo

Hawai'i

Kīlauea is the world's most active volcano. Visitors can enjoy the awesome views.

HIGHEST AND LOWEST POINTS
Highest: Mauna Kea on the island of Hawai'i at 13,796 feet (4,205 m)
Lowest: Sea level along the Pacific Ocean

You're in Hawai'i Volcanoes National Park. Steamy clouds pour out of the ground. Lava, or melted rock, glows fiery red. Stay clear! The lava and steam are dangerous!

Hawai'i is way out in the Pacific Ocean. It's made up of more than 130 islands! There are eight main islands. The biggest is the island of Hawai'i. It's often called the Big Island. The others are O'ahu, Maui, Lāna'i, Kaua'i, Moloka'i, Kaho'olawe, and Ni'ihau. Hawai'i's islands are actually the tops of volcanoes. Lava once poured out of them. The rock cooled and formed the islands. Most of these volcanoes are now **dormant.** But some are still smoking away!

6

Hawai'i Volcanoes National Park is near Hilo on the island of Hawai'i. Its most famous volcanoes are Kīlauea and Mauna Loa.

Highest Temperature: Pāhala on the island of Hawai'i April 27, 1931 100°F (38°C)

Lowest Temperature: Mauna Kea May 17, 1979 12°F (−11°C)

Kaua'i

Ni'ihau

O'ahu

PACIFIC OCEAN

Moloka'i

Lāna'i

Maui

Kaho'olawe

Don't get confused! Hawai'i is a state made up of many islands. One of those islands is also named Hawai'i.

No one lives on the island of Kaho'olawe.

PACIFIC OCEAN

Mauna Kea

Hawai'i   Hilo

Pāhala

Kīlauea is the world's most active volcano.

The bowl-shaped top of a volcano is called a crater.

The island of Kaua'i is known for its "barking sands." When you walk on the beach, the sand sounds like a barking dog!

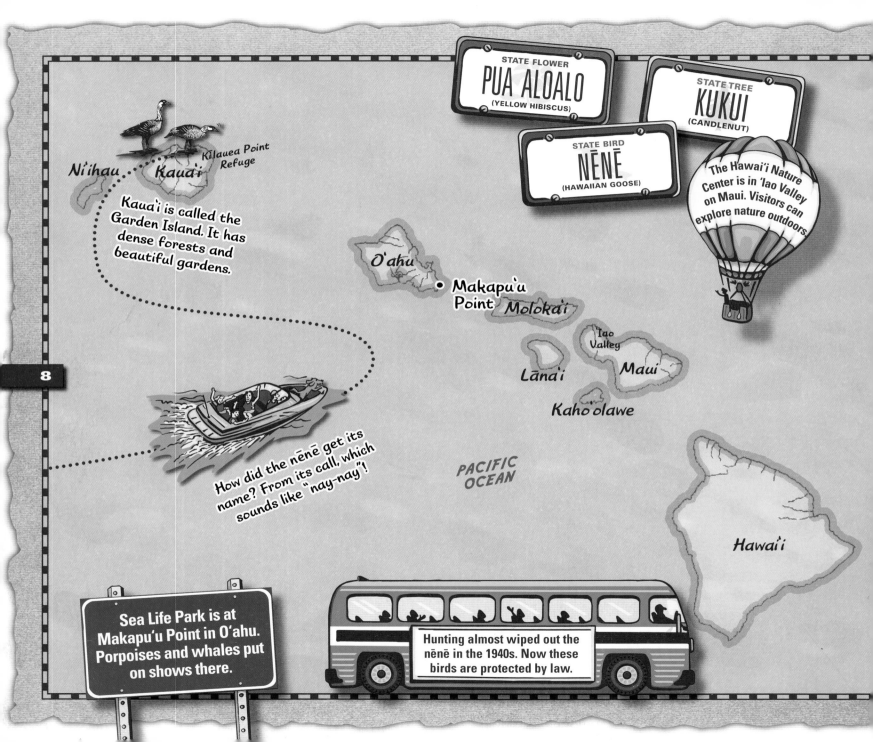

STATE FLOWER
PUA ALOALO
(YELLOW HIBISCUS)

STATE TREE
KUKUI
(CANDLENUT)

STATE BIRD
NĒNĒ
(HAWAIIAN GOOSE)

The Hawai'i Nature Center is in 'Iao Valley on Maui. Visitors can explore nature outdoors.

Kīlauea Point Refuge

Ni'ihau   Kaua'i

Kaua'i is called the Garden Island. It has dense forests and beautiful gardens.

O'ahu

• Makapu'u Point

Moloka'i

'Iao Valley

Lāna'i   Maui

Kaho'olawe

How did the nēnē get its name? From its call, which sounds like "nay-nay"!

PACIFIC OCEAN

Hawai'i

Sea Life Park is at Makapu'u Point in O'ahu. Porpoises and whales put on shows there.

Hunting almost wiped out the nēnē in the 1940s. Now these birds are protected by law.

Y ou're exploring Kīlauea Point National Wildlife Refuge. That's on the north coast of the island of Kaua'i. Suddenly you hear a soft, honking call. It's a nēnē, or Hawaiian goose.

Many seabirds nest along Hawai'i's coasts. Huge sea turtles nest there, too. Whales, seals, and dolphins swim offshore.

Many islands have rugged mountains. Waterfalls plunge down the rocky hillsides. Deep forests stretch for miles. They're home to mongooses, frogs, and lizards.

Many food plants grow wild in Hawai'i. These include papaya, banana, and coconut palm trees. Plumeria and other beautiful flowers are everywhere.

The nēnē is a special bird. It's an endangered species.

The National Park Service has 8 sites in Hawai'i.

9

What a party! Aloha Festivals is Hawai'i's largest festival.

The waves rise higher than a house. They crash with a thundering roar! This is O'ahu's northern coast. The world's biggest surfing contests are held here.

Surfing is a favorite sport in Hawai'i. People love sunning on the beaches, too. Honolulu's Waikīkī Beach is popular for both of these. Honolulu is located on O'ahu's southern coast.

Aloha Festivals is a big event in Hawai'i. It begins in late September. People celebrate with feasts, parades, and **hula** dancing.

Football games bring many visitors to Hawai'i. Maui hosts the Hula Bowl in Wailuku in January. It's a college all-star game. The National Football League's Pro Bowl is in February. It's held in Honolulu's Aloha Stadium.

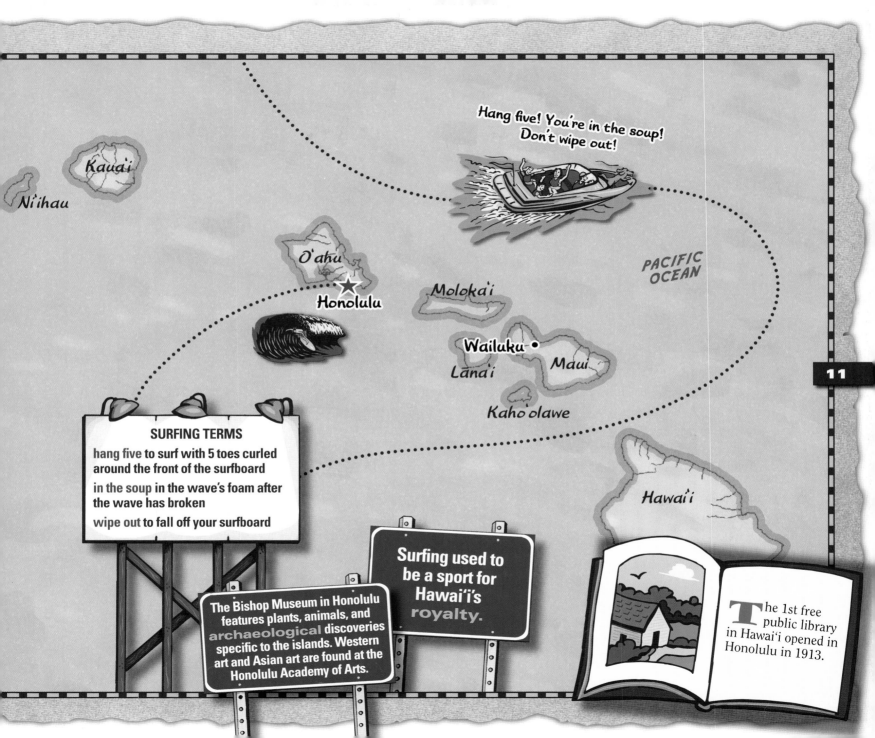

Hang five! You're in the soup! Don't wipe out!

Ni'ihau

Kaua'i

O'ahu

★ Honolulu

PACIFIC OCEAN

Moloka'i

Wailuku •

Lāna'i

Maui

Kaho'olawe

Hawai'i

SURFING TERMS

hang five to surf with 5 toes curled around the front of the surfboard

in the soup in the wave's foam after the wave has broken

wipe out to fall off your surfboard

The Bishop Museum in Honolulu features plants, animals, and **archaeological** discoveries specific to the islands. Western art and Asian art are found at the Honolulu Academy of Arts.

Surfing used to be a sport for Hawai'i's **royalty.**

The 1st free public library in Hawai'i opened in Honolulu in 1913.

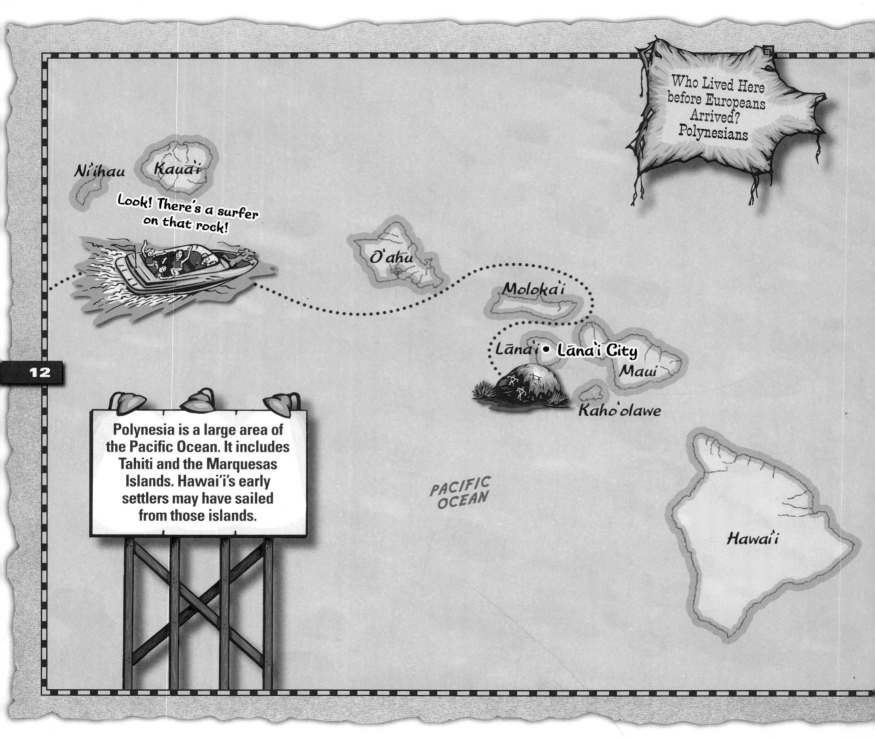

The Luahiwa Petroglyphs on Lāna'i

Climb a certain hillside on the island of Lāna'i. About twenty big rocks are scattered there. They're carved with amazing pictures! There are people, goats, dogs, and turtles. There are scenes of battles and hunts.

These are the Luahiwa Petroglyphs near Lāna'i City. Petroglyphs are words or pictures carved in rock. Early Hawaiians carved them hundreds of years ago.

Polynesians were the first people in Hawai'i. They arrived about 1,500 years ago. They came from faraway islands.

Captain James Cook sailed to Hawai'i in 1778. This British explorer was the first European in Hawai'i. Soon, many other explorers and traders came.

More than 450 carvings are found on the petroglyphs on Lāna'i.

Captain Cook named Hawai'i the Sandwich Islands, after the Earl of Sandwich. Sandwiches were named after him, too!

14

All hail the king! Hawaiians celebrate King Kamehameha Day in Honolulu.

It's a Hawaiian custom to welcome or honor people by draping leis around their necks.

Girls on horseback parade down the street. Everyone's wearing a lei, which is a necklace of flowers. But one figure has more leis than anyone else. It's the statue of King Kamehameha I.

You're in Kapa'au, on the island of Hawai'i. And it's June 11. That's King Kamehameha Day!

King Kamehameha I was a great leader. He united Hawai'i into one kingdom in 1795. Europeans were beginning to explore the islands. But Kamehameha kept his kingdom strong and free.

All of Hawai'i celebrates King Kamehameha Day. People in Kapa'au are very proud that day. The king was born near their town.

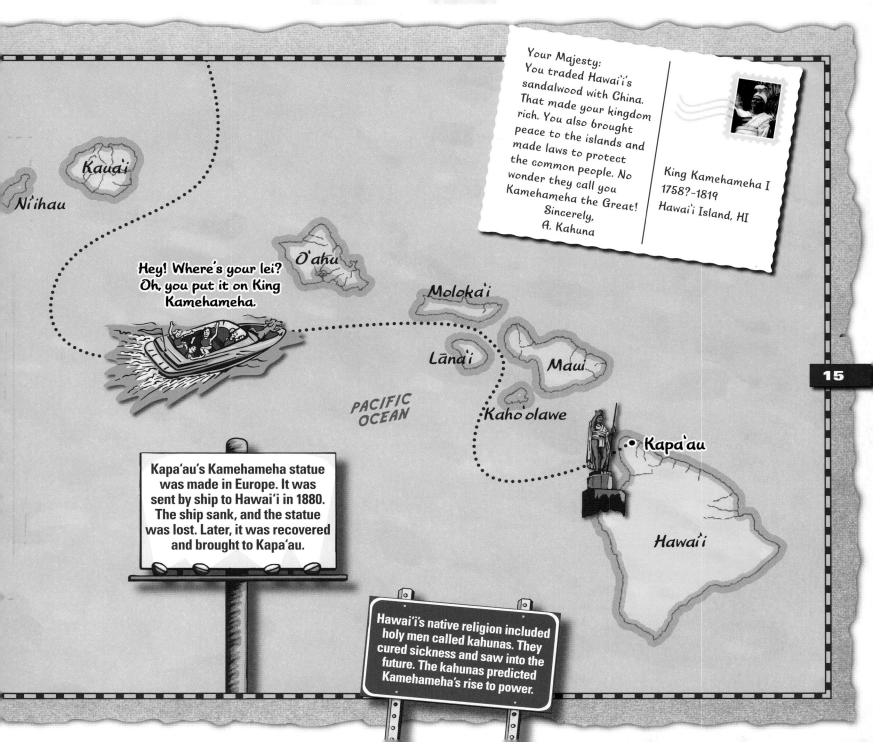

Your Majesty:
You traded Hawai'i's sandalwood with China. That made your kingdom rich. You also brought peace to the islands and made laws to protect the common people. No wonder they call you Kamehameha the Great!
Sincerely,
A. Kahuna

King Kamehameha I
1758?-1819
Hawai'i Island, HI

Ni'ihau

Kaua'i

O'ahu

Moloka'i

Hey! Where's your lei? Oh, you put it on King Kamehameha.

Lāna'i

Maui

PACIFIC OCEAN

Kaho'olawe

Kapa'au

Kapa'au's Kamehameha statue was made in Europe. It was sent by ship to Hawai'i in 1880. The ship sank, and the statue was lost. Later, it was recovered and brought to Kapa'au.

Hawai'i

Hawai'i's native religion included holy men called kahunas. They cured sickness and saw into the future. The kahunas predicted Kamehameha's rise to power.

You see stone lamps and coconut graters. You see fishhooks made of seashells. You see curved poi boards, too. Hawaiians pounded cooked taro root on these boards. That's how they made a food called poi.

You're visiting Hāna Cultural Center on Maui. It **preserves** an early Hawaiian community. Several *hale,* or houses, stand there. They show much about Hawaiian life in the 1800s.

Protestant **missionaries** arrived in 1820. They taught many Hawaiians about Christianity. The Hawaiians' way of life changed. They began to dress like Americans and Europeans. But they also kept some ancient customs. Many new settlers adopted Hawaiian customs, too.

Learn about the history of the Hawaiian people. Discover the past at the Hāna Cultural Center.

This is the stuff I put on cereal? Raw sugar comes from sugarcane stalks.

Gay and Robinson Sugar Plantation on Kaua'i

Take a tour of Gay and Robinson Sugar Plantation in Kaumakani. It's a huge farm on the island of Kaua'i. You'll see acres of sugarcane plants. You'll see a sugar factory, too. It turns sugarcane into molasses and raw sugar.

Americans and Europeans started Hawai'i's first plantations. They opened sugarcane plantations in the 1830s. Pineapple plantations were opened in the 1880s.

Queen Lili'uokalani came to power in 1891. But planters and other foreigners were powerful, too. They led a revolution in 1893. Lili'uokalani was removed from the throne. Then Hawai'i became the Republic of Hawai'i. It became a U.S. territory in 1900.

Sugarcane stalks are pressed to squeeze out a thick, sweet juice. That juice yields molasses and raw sugar.

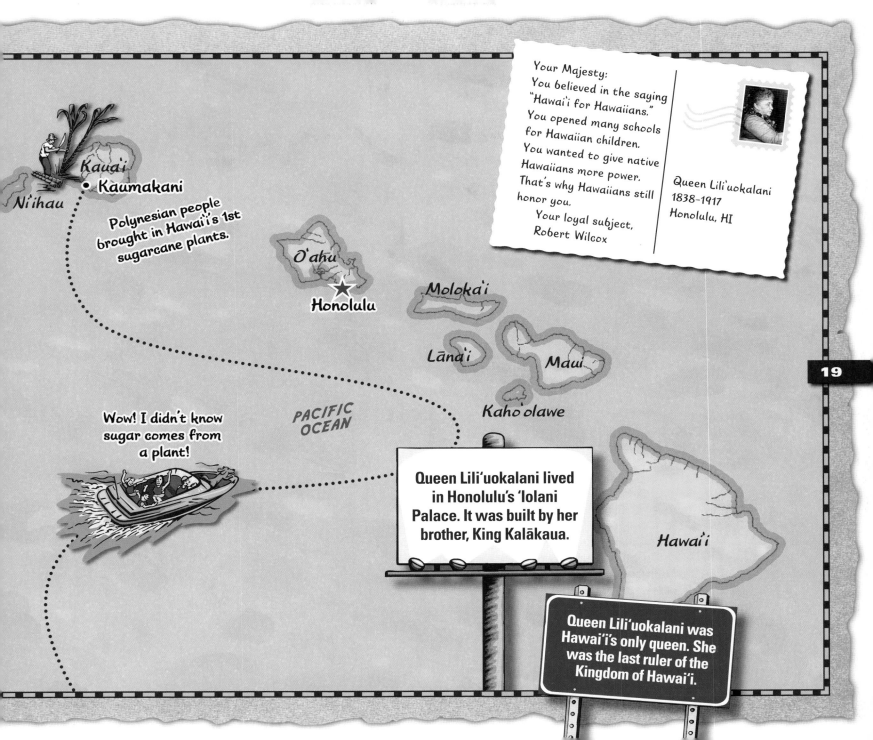

Kaua'i

• **Kaumakani**

Ni'ihau

Polynesian people brought in Hawai'i's 1st sugarcane plants.

O'ahu

★
Honolulu

Moloka'i

Lāna'i

Maui

Kaho'olawe

PACIFIC OCEAN

Hawai'i

Wow! I didn't know sugar comes from a plant!

Queen Lili'uokalani lived in Honolulu's 'Iolani Palace. It was built by her brother, King Kalākaua.

Queen Lili'uokalani was Hawai'i's only queen. She was the last ruler of the Kingdom of Hawai'i.

Your Majesty:
You believed in the saying "Hawai'i for Hawaiians."
You opened many schools for Hawaiian children.
You wanted to give native Hawaiians more power.
That's why Hawaiians still honor you.
    Your loyal subject,
    Robert Wilcox

Queen Lili'uokalani
1838–1917
Honolulu, HI

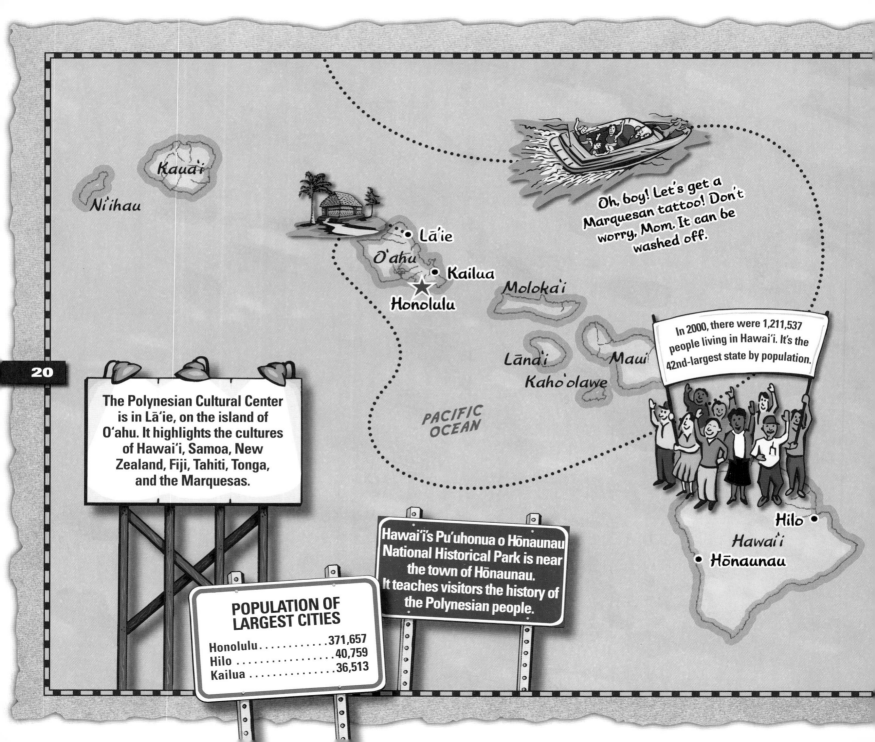

Kaua'i

Ni'ihau

Lā'ie

O'ahu

Kailua

Honolulu

Moloka'i

Lāna'i

Kaho'olawe

Maui

PACIFIC OCEAN

Hilo

Hawai'i

Hōnaunau

Oh, boy! Let's get a Marquesan tattoo! Don't worry, Mom. It can be washed off.

In 2000, there were 1,211,537 people living in Hawai'i. It's the 42nd-largest state by population.

The Polynesian Cultural Center is in Lā'ie, on the island of O'ahu. It highlights the cultures of Hawai'i, Samoa, New Zealand, Fiji, Tahiti, Tonga, and the Marquesas.

Hawai'i's Pu'uhonua o Hōnaunau National Historical Park is near the town of Hōnaunau. It teaches visitors the history of the Polynesian people.

POPULATION OF LARGEST CITIES

Honolulu 371,657
Hilo 40,759
Kailua 36,513

The Polynesian Cultural Center on O'ahu

I hope I get a bite! These kids are learning about Tahitian fishing.

Toss a spear and crack a coconut. Try an ancient form of bowling. You're at the Polynesian Cultural Center! It has many villages. Each one features the **culture** of a Polynesian island.

Polynesian people were the first Hawaiians. Hawaiians developed their own language. Today, many Hawaiian words are still used in Hawai'i. Native Hawaiian food and music are common, too.

Now people from many **ethnic** groups live in Hawai'i. Planters brought in **immigrants** to work their farms. These workers came from China, Japan, Portugal, and other lands. They all brought different customs with them. Now these customs are part of Hawaiian life.

O'ahu has the highest population of all the islands. It's home to about 3 out of 4 people in Hawai'i.

Macadamia nuts are an important crop in Hawai'i. They're delicious, too!

Hawai'i grows 9 out of every 10 of the world's macadamia nuts.

Put that macadamia nut in a sock. That way, you won't hurt your fingers. Then smash it with a hammer. Whack!

You're visiting Purdy's Macadamia Nut Farm. It's near Kualapu'u on the island of Moloka'i. The Purdys are happy to show you around. They'll teach you stuff, too. Like how to crack a macadamia nut!

People in Hawai'i grow lots of unusual crops. Pineapple and sugarcane are the major crops. They mostly grow on the island of Maui.

Farmers also raise nuts, coffee, and flowers. Many delicious fruits grow in Hawai'i, too. Bananas, mangoes, and papayas are just a few. And you don't need a hammer to eat them!

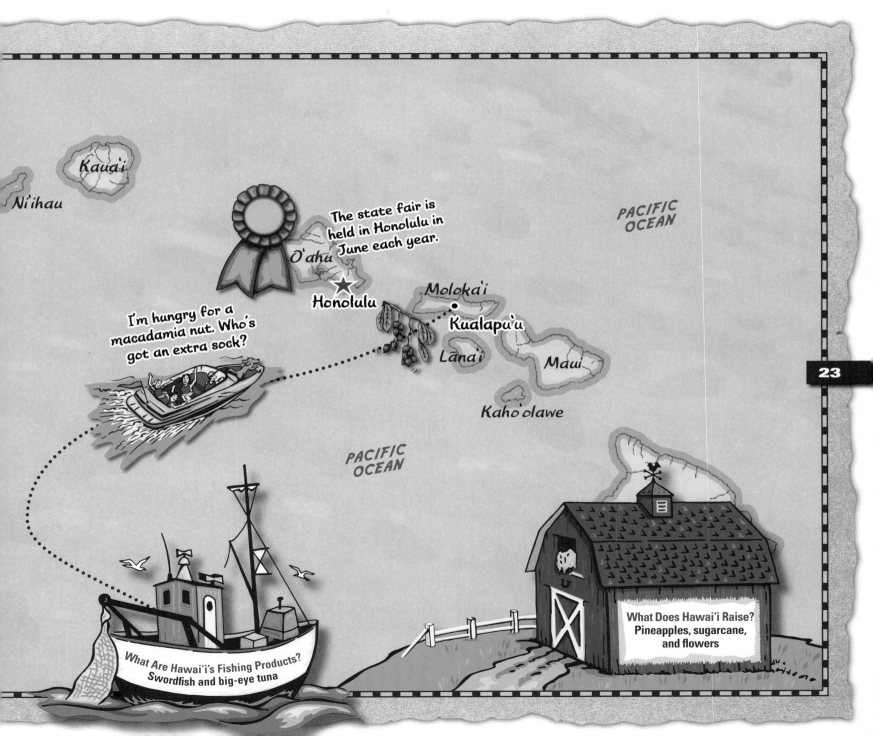

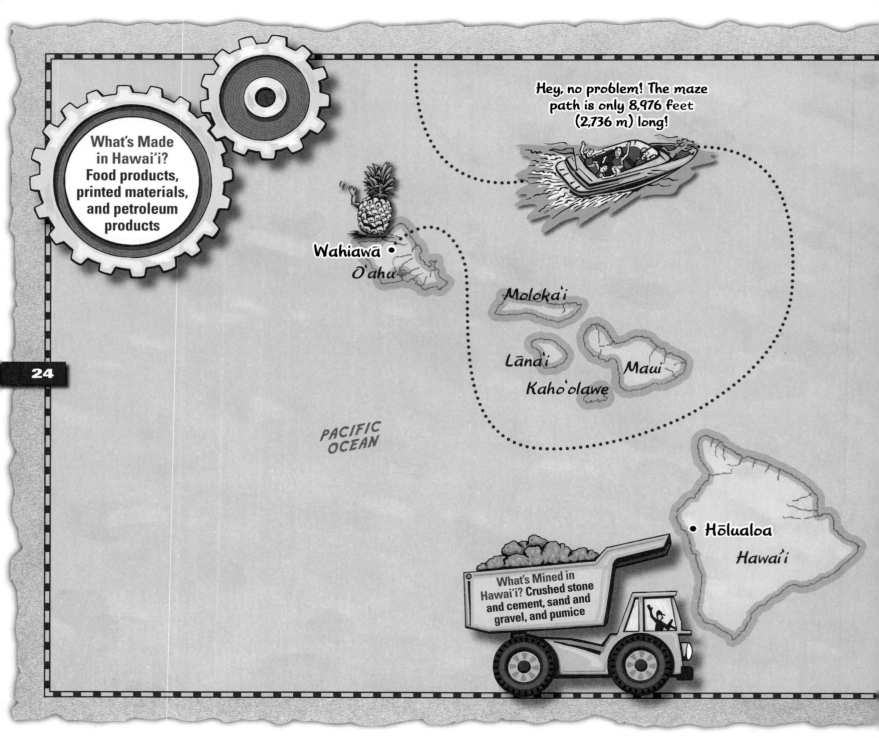

What's Made in Hawai'i? Food products, printed materials, and petroleum products

Hey, no problem! The maze path is only 8,976 feet (2,736 m) long!

Wahiawā •
O'ahu

Moloka'i

Lāna'i
Kaho'olawe
Maui

PACIFIC OCEAN

• Hōlualoa
Hawai'i

What's Mined in Hawai'i? Crushed stone and cement, sand and gravel, and pumice

24

Dole Plantation's Pineapple Garden Maze

Turn left, turn right, go straight. Oops! A dead end!

You're at Dole Plantation near Wahiawā on O'ahu. Farmers there grow pineapples. And you're in the Pineapple Garden **Maze.** It's the biggest maze in the world. Don't get lost!

You can tour this plantation in a little train. You'll see its store, too. It's full of pineapple products.

Foods are Hawai'i's major factory products. Crops such as pineapples go from farms to factories. There they might be squeezed, chopped, or cooked. Sugarcane ends up as sugar. Fruits become fruit juice, soft drinks, or jam. Some crops end up as candy. Yum!

This place is amazing! I hope we can find our way out.

Looking for a plantation and factory tour? Check out Kona Coffee Company at Hōlualoa on the island of Hawai'i.

The *Arizona* Memorial Museum at Pearl Harbor

Visitors can tour the *Arizona* Memorial Museum. They remember those who died in 1941.

Look down through the clear blue water. You can see a sunken ship down there. It's the battleship USS *Arizona*.

You're visiting the *Arizona* Memorial Museum. It's at Pearl Harbor on the island of O'ahu. Japan bombed the U.S. base there in 1941. The *Arizona* sank, and many people died. Then the United States entered World War II (1939–1945).

Hawai'i grew quickly after the war. Tourism became a big business. Now millions of people visit Hawai'i every year. They enjoy the state's natural beauty and warm climate.

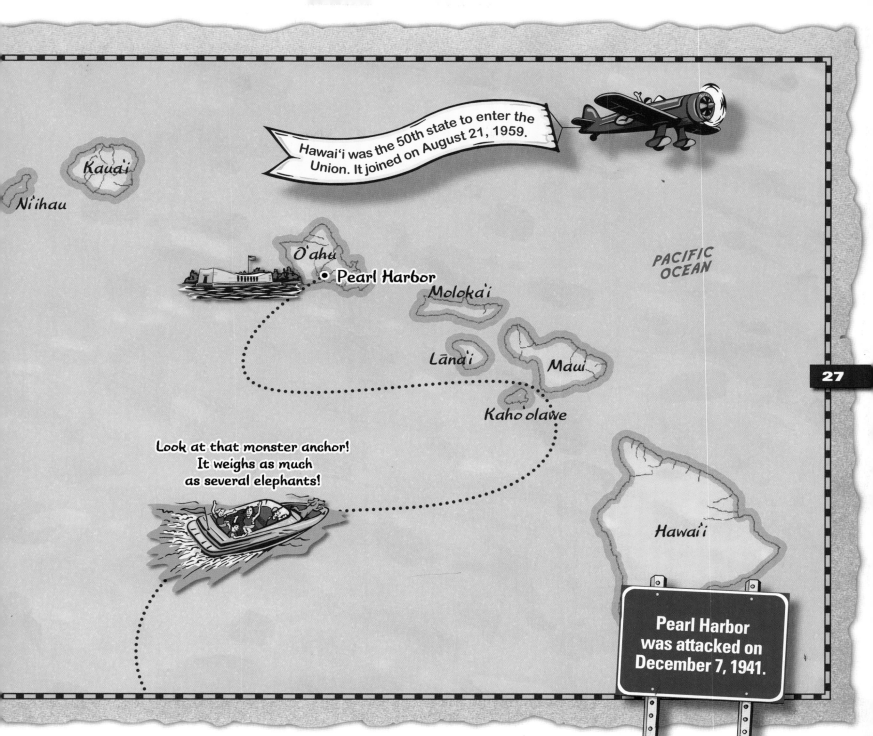

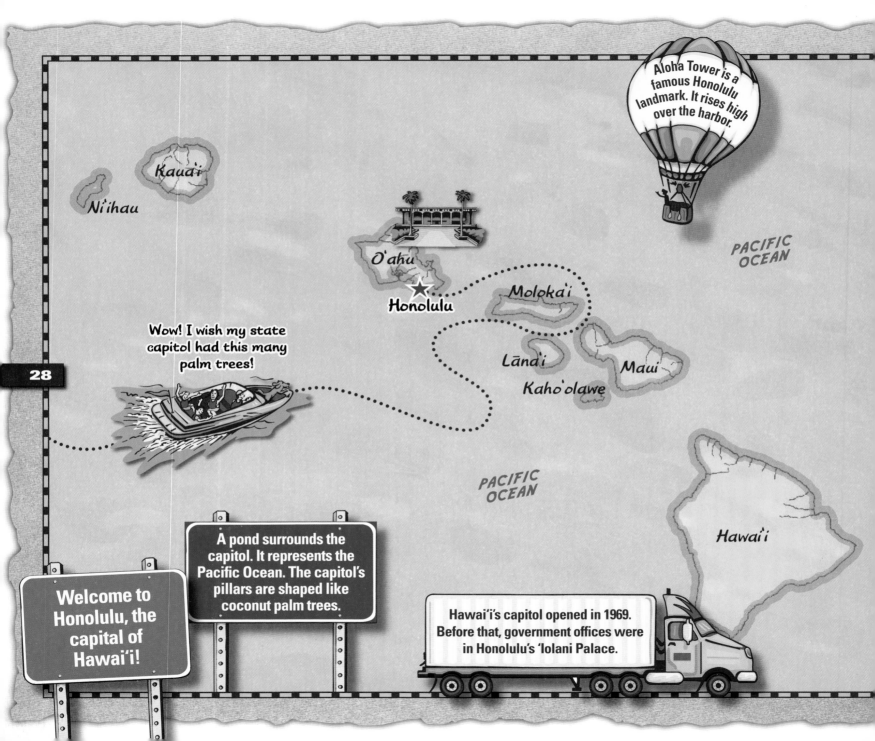

Aloha Tower is a famous Honolulu landmark. It rises high over the harbor.

PACIFIC OCEAN

Kaua'i

Ni'ihau

O'ahu

★
Honolulu

Moloka'i

Lāna'i

Kaho'olawe

Maui

Wow! I wish my state capitol had this many palm trees!

PACIFIC OCEAN

Hawai'i

A pond surrounds the capitol. It represents the Pacific Ocean. The capitol's pillars are shaped like coconut palm trees.

Welcome to Honolulu, the capital of Hawai'i!

Hawai'i's capitol opened in 1969. Before that, government offices were in Honolulu's 'Iolani Palace.

Y ou've never seen a state capitol like Hawai'i's. It was built with a volcano in mind! The top is open to the sky. That's what craters look like. Some rooms are cone-shaped—just like volcanoes. What a great home for state government offices!

Wow, check out the state capitol! It's really cool and different!

Hawai'i's state government has three branches. One branch makes laws for the state. The governor heads another branch. It makes sure people obey the laws. Judges make up the third branch. They decide whether laws have been broken.

29

Hawai'i's state motto is *Ua Mau Ke Ea O Ka 'Āina I Ka Pono.* This is Hawaiian for "The Life of the Land Is Perpetuated in Righteousness."

Haleakalā National Park is a natural wonder. Be sure to visit at sunrise!

30

Y ou're hiking up Haleakalā volcano. It's very early in the morning. You're bundled up because it's so cold. Suddenly, rays of light burst out. The Sun has risen!

Haleakalā is Hawaiian for "house of the Sun." People like to drive to the top of this volcano at sunrise. They watch the sky turn beautiful colors.

At the top, you'll explore the crater. It's the largest crater in the world. Hiking across it can take many days!

Ancient Hawaiian legends say that the Sun sleeps in Haleakalā's giant crater.

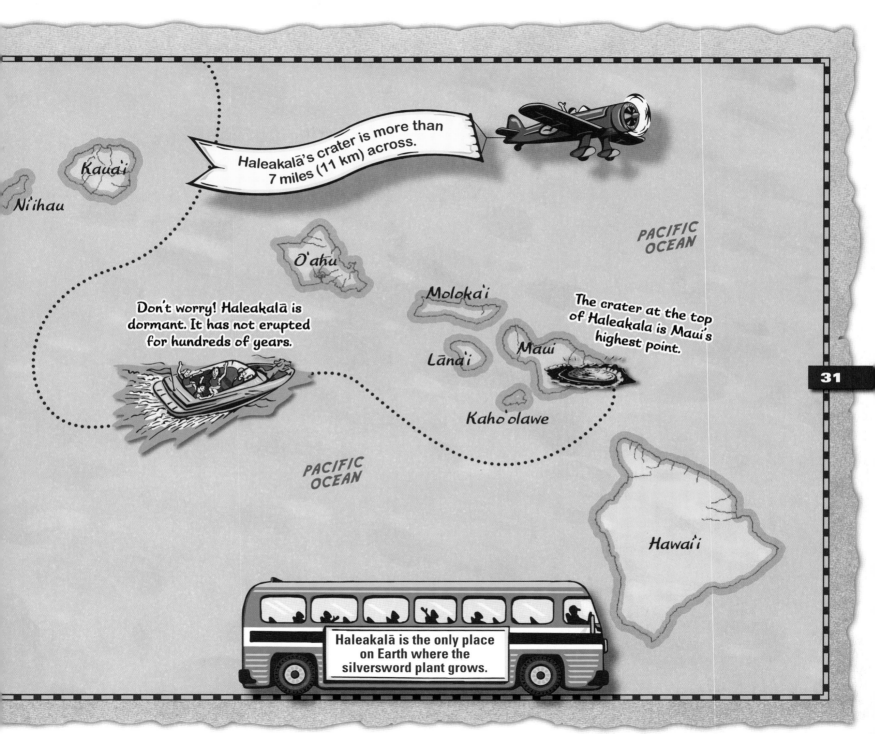

Haleakalā's crater is more than 7 miles (11 km) across.

Don't worry! Haleakalā is dormant. It has not erupted for hundreds of years.

The crater at the top of Haleakala is Maui's highest point.

Haleakalā is the only place on Earth where the silversword plant grows.

PACIFIC OCEAN

PACIFIC OCEAN

Ni'ihau

Kaua'i

O'ahu

Moloka'i

Lāna'i

Maui

Kaho'olawe

Hawai'i

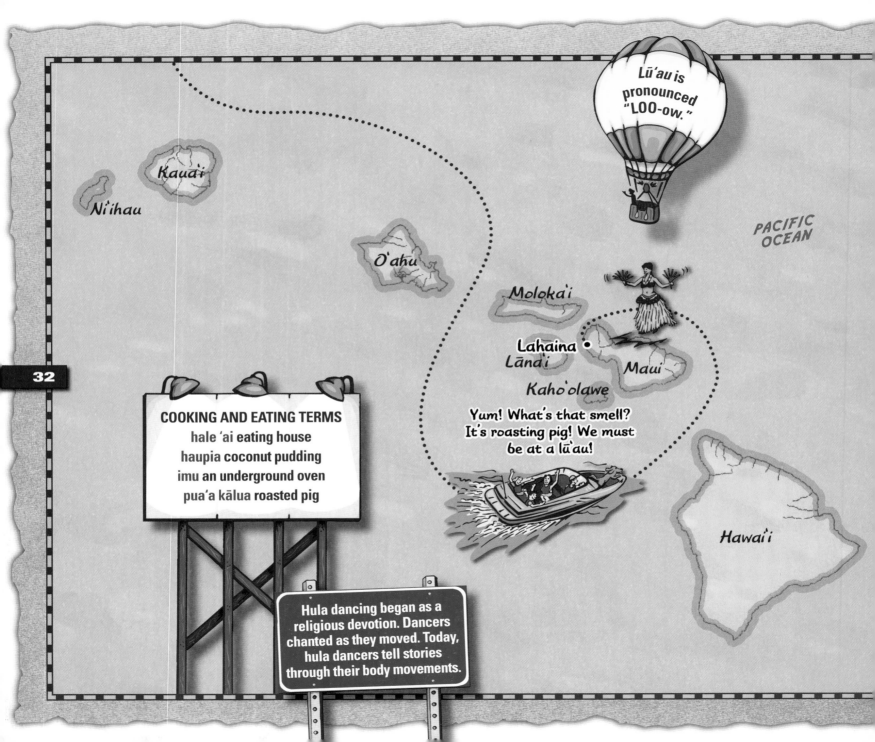

Lū'au is pronounced "LOO-ow."

PACIFIC OCEAN

Ni'ihau

Kaua'i

O'ahu

Moloka'i

Lahaina •
Lāna'i

Maui

Kaho'olawe

Yum! What's that smell?
It's roasting pig! We must
be at a lū'au!

Hawai'i

COOKING AND EATING TERMS
hale 'ai eating house
haupia coconut pudding
imu an underground oven
pua'a kālua roasted pig

Hula dancing began as a
religious devotion. Dancers
chanted as they moved. Today,
hula dancers tell stories
through their body movements.

A Lūʻau at Lahaina

Tables of food seem to stretch for miles. They're loaded with chicken, salmon, and squid. There's every color of fruit and vegetable. In the middle is a big roasted pig.

You're enjoying a lūʻau. That's a huge Hawaiian feast. This one's at Lahaina on Maui's west coast. Its lūʻaus are famous.

Big feasts are an old Hawaiian **tradition.** They were held to celebrate special events. Today's lūʻaus usually include a show. There are hula dances with traditional music. There may be Samoan fire knife dances. Some shows tell the history of the Hawaiian people. So a lūʻau is much more than just a meal!

Hula dancers are a traditional part of lūʻaus. Lūʻaus are both fun and educational!

Lūʻau is the Hawaiian word for "taro plant leaves." Traditionally, these leaves are wrapped around various foods and then steamed.

33

Riding Mules on the Cliffs of Moloka'i

Just hop on your mule and go! People love to ride mules to Kalaupapa.

The Hawaiian government began sending people with Hansen's disease to Moloka'i in 1866.

Your mule's name is Friendly. But you wish his name were Steady. You're riding him along Moloka'i's northern cliffs. They're the highest sea cliffs in the world!

Soon you reach the village of Kalaupapa. It was once a village for sick people. They all had Hansen's disease. A priest called Father Damien cared for them. Many people were afraid they would catch the disease. But Father Damien was brave. The sick people loved him for his kindness.

Now you're back on your mule. This time, you're not afraid. Friendly is very steady on those cliffs!

Hansen's disease affects the skin, nerves, and muscles. It can now be cured with medicine. Hansen's disease used to be called leprosy.

Kaua'i

Ni'ihau

O'ahu

Mules are animals whose parents are a horse and a donkey.

Kalaupapa •

Moloka'i

Are you sure this mule knows what it's doing? It's mighty far down to the sea!

Lāna'i

Maui

Kaho'olawe

PACIFIC OCEAN

Guides who manage the mules are called mule skinners.

Father Damien was a Roman Catholic priest from Belgium. His full name was Joseph Damien de Veuster. He came to Kalaupapa in 1873.

Dear Father Damien: People with Hansen's disease were treated badly. No one wanted to be near them. But you helped ease their pain. Then you died of the disease yourself. What a good person you were!
Sincerely,
An Admirer

Father Damien
1840-1889
Kalaupapa, Moloka'i

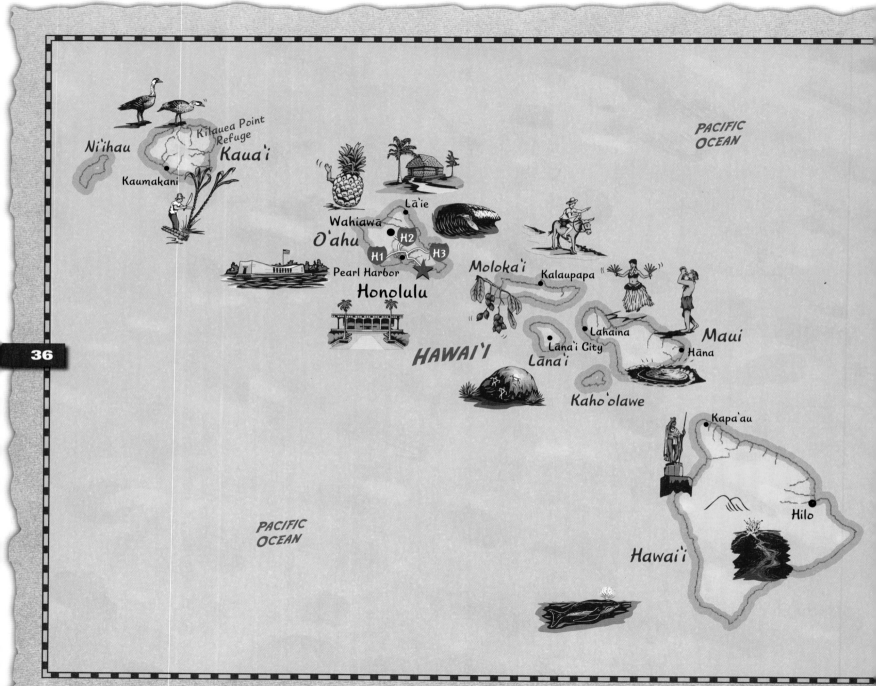

PACIFIC
OCEAN

Ni'ihau

Kilauea Point
Refuge

Kaua'i

Kaumakani

Lā'ie

Wahiawā

O'ahu

H2

H1

H3

Pearl Harbor

Honolulu

Moloka'i

Kalaupapa

HAWAI'I

Lāna'i City

Lāna'i

Lahaina

Maui

Hāna

Kaho'olawe

Kapa'au

Hilo

Hawai'i

PACIFIC
OCEAN

OUR TRIP

We visited many places on our trip! We also met a lot of interesting people along the way. Look at the map on the left. Use your finger to trace all the places we have been.

Which island has "barking sand"? See page 7 for the answer.

Which islands does Polynesia include? Page 12 has the answer.

What is poi? See page 16 for the answer.

Who was Hawai'i's only queen? Look on page 19 for the answer.

How many macadamia nuts does Hawai'i grow? Page 22 has the answer.

When was Pearl Harbor attacked? Turn to page 27 for the answer.

Where does the silversword plant grow? Look on page 31 and find out!

What is another name for Hansen's disease? Turn to page 35 for the answer.

That was a great trip! We have traveled all over Hawai'i!

There are a few places that we didn't have time for, though. Next time, we plan to visit the Pacific Tsunami Museum in Hilo. This museum educates visitors about giant and destructive sea waves. It features exhibits on tsunami safety and the history of tsunamis in Hawai'i.

More Places to Visit in Hawai'i

WORDS TO KNOW

archaeological (AR-kee-uh-LA-juh-kuhl) relating to the study of the remains of past cultures

culture (KUHL-chur) a people's customs, beliefs, and way of life

dormant (DOR-muhnt) not active; sleeping

ethnic (ETH-nik) relating to a race or nationality

hula (HOO-luh) a Hawaiian dance performed with swaying movements

immigrants (IM-uh-gruhntz) people who move from their homeland to a new land

legends (LEJ-uhndz) old tales created to explain something

maze (MAYZ) a confusing set of pathways

missionaries (MISH-uh-ner-eez) people who travel to spread their religion

preserves (pri-ZURVZ) protects something so that it remains unchanged

royalty (ROI-uhl-tee) kings, queens, and other nobles

tradition (truh-DISH-uhn) custom

volcano (vol-KAY-noh) a mountain that releases steam and melted rock

Hawai'i covers 6,423 square miles (16,635 sq km). It's the 47th-largest state in size.

STATE SYMBOLS

State bird: Nēnē (Hawaiian goose)

State dance: Hula

State fish: Humuhumunukunukuāpua'a (rectangular triggerfish)

State flower: Pua aloalo (yellow hibiscus)

State gem: Black coral

State individual sport: Surfing

State marine mammal: Humpback whale

State team sport: Outrigger canoe paddling

State tree: Kukui (candlenut)

State flag

State seal

STATE SONG

"Hawai'i Pono'ī" ("Hawai'i's Own")

Words by King David Kalākaua, music by Henry Berger

In Hawaiian:
Hawai'i pono'ī
Nānā i kou, mō'ī
Ka lani ali'i,
Ke ali'i.

Hui:
Makua lani ē,
Kamehameha ē,
Nā kaua e pale,
Me ka ihe.

Hawai'i pono'ī
Nānā i nā ali'i
Nā pua muli kou
Nā pōki'i.

Hawai'i pono'ī
E ka lāhui e
'O kāu hana nui
E ui e.

In English:
Hawai'i's own true sons
Be loyal to your chief
Your country's liege and lord
The chief.

Chorus:
Royal father
Kamehameha
Shall defend in war
With spears.

Hawai'i's own true sons
Look to your chief
Those chiefs of younger birth
Younger descent.

Hawai'i's own true sons
People of loyal heart
The only duty lies
List and abide.

FAMOUS PEOPLE

Ariyoshi, George (1926–), governor

Atisanoe, Salevaa (Konishiki) (1963–), sumo wrestler

Bingham, Hiram (1789–1869), missionary

Carrere, Tia (1967–), actor

de Veuster, Joseph Damien (1840–1889), missionary

Fong, Hiram L. (1906–2004), senator

Ho, Don (1930–), singer

Kahanamoku, Duke Paoa (1890–1968), Olympic swimmer, surfing pioneer

Kamakawiwoʻole, Israel (1959–1997), singer

Kidman, Nicole (1967–), actor

Liliʻuokalani, Queen Lydia (1838–1917), Hawaiian queen

Lowry, Lois (1937–), children's author

Midler, Bette (1945–), singer, actor

Onizuka, Ellison S. (1946–1986), astronaut

Sakata, Harold (1920–1982), actor

Shigeta, James (1933–), actor

Stroud, Don (1943–), actor

Tuttle, Merlin (1941 –), mammalogist

Wie, Michelle (1989–), golfer

TO FIND OUT MORE

At the Library

Hayashi, Leslie Ann, and Kathleen Wong Bishop (illustrator). *Fables from the Sea.* Honolulu: University of Hawaiʻi, 2000.

Stamper, Judith Bauer, and John Speirs (illustrator). *Voyage to the Volcano.* New York: Scholastic, 2003.

Takayama, Sandi, and Pat Hall (illustrator). *The Musubi Man: Hawaiʻi's Gingerbread Man.* Honolulu: Bess Press, 1996.

Williams, Julie Stewart, and Robin Yoko Racoma (illustrator). *From the Mountains to the Sea: A Hawaiian Lifestyle.* Honolulu: Kamehameha Schools Press, 1997.

On the Web

Visit our home page for lots of links about Hawaiʻi:
http://www.childsworld.com/links

Note to Parents, Teachers, and Librarians: We routinely verify our Web links to make sure they are safe, active sites—so encourage your readers to check them out!

Places to Visit or Contact

Hawaiian Historical Society
560 Kawaiahaʻo Street
Honolulu, HI 96813
808/537-6271
For more information about the history of Hawaiʻi

Hawaiʻi Visitors and Convention Bureau
2270 Kalākaua Avenue,
Suite 801
Honolulu, HI 96815
808/923-1811
For more information about traveling in Hawaiʻi

INDEX

Bye, Aloha State.
We had a great time.
We'll come back soon!